Images of
CARDIFF

Images of
CARDIFF

First published in Great Britain in 1995 by The Breedon Books Publishing Company Limited Breedon House, 44 Friar Gate, Derby, DE1 1DA. Reprinted in paperback 2005.

This paperback reprint published in Great Britain in 2011 by The Derby Books Publishing Company Limited, 3 The Parker Centre, Mansfield Road, Derby DE21 4SZ.

ISBN 978-1-85983-866-2

Printed and bound by Melita Press, Malta.

CONTENTS

INTRODUCTION

AS THEY say, the Past is another country …here is your passport to carry you into it. It takes you across the frontiers of Time, spinning you back to a land that might have been lost forever but for the skills of our first intrepid explorers – those cameramen who went out to catch Cardiff in all its incarnations, freezing on film for all time the milestones of our century.

We have reached into our library, plundered their pictures to rebuild slices of the city obliterated long, long ago. Legendary games are replayed on these pages; we meet the All Blacks of other days once more, exult again in City's FA Cup triumph of 1927 and share the joy that came with Glamorgan's County Championships.

Here are children at play in streets long lost, who grew, to share the city's triumphs and disasters, who reached old age, who vanished like the streets – to be born again in these pages, the camera offering the secret of perpetual youth.

Cardiff today stands at the threshold of greatness. The city has been transformed and there is more, much more to come.

But this bright and brave New World, the world of Now, is founded on a world of Then. And that is the world within these pages.

If you like, think of it as a sort of archaeology, stripping away the surface, layer by layer, to reveal the cities – yes, cities, for there have been many Cardiffs – that once sprouted around the Castle and its river. And, of course, we show the men and the women and the children who made this city home, and the men and the women, Winston Churchill, Kings and Queens among them, who became, briefly, a part of our history on certain, shining days.

The camera came too late to capture the Cardiff of Norman times. What a subject the building of our Castle or Llandaff Cathedral would have made. We missed the birth of the railways that triggered our first phenomenal growth. But we were lucky – it got here in time to chart the rise – and fall – of the mighty docks, to catch the flow, then the ebb of the Glamorganshire Canal, the sprouting of factories, and furnaces that blazed like beacons to bring in more men who would, in time, raise families and become … Cardiffians.

What a century it's been. From horsedrawn cab to elegant coach and trains running at unimaginable speeds. From flickering gaslight to sunlight on tall standards. From music-hall to cinema and, then TV with radio, or wireless as they knew it, opening wider windows to the world.

We chart their passage, and they are all here, in your passport to that other country. Old men, old women might remember the little streets and the buildings of Then. Some of them might even be the children who played in those streets. But for today's children, and their parents, perhaps, this book is truly a guide to another country. Our Past.

Perhaps they can share with their forebears the wonder felt when the airship built in Cardiff by Ernest Willows glided over the five-year-old City Hall in 1910.

And sense the traumas felt when other aircraft came to the city in 1941, to bring the darkest days of our history, to kill and maim, and shatter the small streets.

To look at the pictures of the destruction makes it easy to understand the joy when the little streets that survived shook off the traumas, to celebrate. The joy springs up from the pages.

And here are our heroes. Some now ghosts that stalk these pages.

Peerless Jim Driscoll, Joe Erskine, the great Paulo Radmilovic, who swam for Britain in six consecutive Olympic Games. And all those other swimmers who splashed gloriously in the river that shaped our city, when the Taff Swim saw the banks packed like the terrace of the Arms Park when the All Blacks visited. Heroes, too, who are still among us, the giants of rugby and soccer and cricket. The boxers and the athletes.

She's silenced forever, now. But you can hear the music when Tessie O'Shea, our own Two Ton Tessie, looks up from these pages. Shirley Bassey, as well. And Tom Jones, a Ponty boy but borrowed and why not?

And so much more …

If a picture's worth a thousand words, then here is your Encyclopaedia of Cardiff.

And remember, in a century or so our own times will be another country to the people living then. We and the city we inhabit will be, to them, what everything in this book is to us.

WAR AND PEACE

The 20th century was punctuated by war, including two world wars in which Wales played a major role. This book begins with some pictures reflecting the joys and sadness of war and peace. And we start with a visit to Cardiff by the wartime Prime Minister, Winston Churchill.

Churchill came on a morale-boosting visit to Cardiff after the blitz which devastated parts of the city in 1941.

Churchill's hat trick outside the City Hall on the visit.

Churchill and his wife Clementine visited blitz victims at Cardiff Royal Infirmary where they were welcomed by hospital chairman Henry Smith, Dr Armstrong and the matron.

Pack up your troubles in your old kit bag . . .Women porters at Cardiff Central with the kitbags of Private Dunn, of Cardiff and Private T.Morgan of Caerphilly as they arrived home from a Japanese Prisoner-of-War camp in 1945.

Lt D.G.Bruce, of Plasturton Gardens, was greeted by his parents when he was the first man from a Japanese Prisoner-of-War camp to reach Cardiff after being repatriated by

All smiles for Bombardier M.Simins, of Cardiff, when he arrived back from a prison camp in the Far East.

All smiles for Bombardier M.Simins, of Cardiff, when he arrived back from a prison camp in the Far East. Corporal Graham Price, of Grangetown, arrived home from a PoW camp in the Far East on his 29th birthday in 1945. His dad carried his kitbag.

A young girl was at Cardiff Central to greet her dad when he was returned from Japan in 1945. The names on the photograph are not clear, but the lance-corporals were both from Treorchy.

Glad to be home… another group of ex-prisoners arriving home from the Far East.

Canton men Sgt W.E.Petrier and Gunner Cornell, wearing an Australian hat, were among this group of ex-prisoners.

Welcome at Cardiff Central for P.Guppy (Merthyr), L.Powell (Porthcawl), J.Hopkins (Mountain Ash).

Sgt T.O. Jones, of Gilfach, with his wife and child, and Gunner P. Hurley, of Senghenydd.

A welcome home lunch for the Cardiff men who were Prisoners-of-War in Japan where their basic diet had been rice and water.

Sgt James Dunne, who was a prisoner in Germany, with his happy parents in Cardiff in 1943. No reason was given on the censored photograph for his early repatriation.

Sgt Dunne is second left in the front of another group of ex-prisoners on their return to Cardiff in 1943. Also in the picture are back row: E.Sullivan, T.Williams, C.H.Thomas, E.Ramell, A.E.Warren. Front row: I.Owen, J.Dunne, Col A.G.Lyttelton, Capt Smith and E.Flynn.

A rare photograph of a Welsh football team, taken at a German PoW camp at Stammlager in 1942. The only one named on the photograph was Private Harold Lemon, of Tonna, Neath (first left, back row).

Mrs D.G.Fletcher, president of the Cardiff Ladies' Social Union with some of the repatriated prisoners at the YMCA, in Station Terrace, Cardiff.

South Wales was targeted by German bombers during World War Two, with the first heavy raids taking place on 2 and 3 January 1941. A land-mine landed at the rear of the Conservative Club in Neville Street, Riverside, leaving many people dead and this scene of devastation.

Many victims of the blitz are buried in unmarked graves in Cathays and Western Cemetery. This was the scene at the graveside in Cathays in January 1941. Thirty-three people are buried where they died when a bomb scored a direct hit on a community shelter at Hollyman's bakery in Corporation Road, Grangetown.

Houses in Albany Road took a direct hit on 3 March 1941.

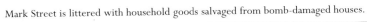

Mark Street is littered with household goods salvaged from bomb-damaged houses.

Once proud homes on the corner of Croft Street and Rose Street were flattened in a raid.

Shocked residents outside a bomb-damaged house off Newport Road.

Llandaff Cathedral was damaged by a land-mine in January 1941. Two months later St David's Cathedral was destroyed by fire bombs.

Pupils at a St Illtyd's School, Cardiff, helped with salvaging items after the school was bombed.

This was the scene after a raid on Fairwater.

Within 24 hours of the famous Dambuster raid on Germany on 17 May 1943, the Germans carried out a revenge attack on Cardiff, killing 43 people. Cardiff was chosen because the leader of the Dambuster Squadron was Wing Commander Guy Gibson, seen here with his Penarth-born wife, Eva Turner. Gibson was in Penarth when he heard he had been awarded the VC.

German pilots were issued with aerial guide books to key targets in Wales, which Kuhnemann helped to compile. The Queen Alexandra Dock was hit by German bombs.

Terry Pasley was only two when he and his mother were dug out of the ruins of their house in St Agnes Road, Heath, Cardiff, destroyed in a raid in May 1943. Here he is pictured 50 years later with his mum and his teddy bear, which was also brought out from the rubble.

Spiller's Flour Mills took a direct hit.

The meat market on the corner of Wharton Street was bombed.

King George VI and Queen Elizabeth came to Cardiff after the blitz in 1941 and were greeted by the Lord Mayor, and young civil defence workers.

Children cheer the Royal visitors.

Members of the Home Guard, 'Dad's Army', on parade at the Arms Park and being inspected by their commander, local solicitor Gerald Gaskell.

Rhiwbina pupils took gas masks to school after war was declared on 3 September 1939.

Home Guard heroes stationed at Llanishen, Cardiff, dealt with a number of delayed action bombs which were dropped on Cardiff in 1941. Len Ackerman, Cliff Dunne, Jonnie Evans and Horace Adey are seen with one of the monsters.

Collecting a land-mine which fell on Cardiff in 1941. The photograph was taken by Leslie Fisher, who drove the break down truck.

Madam Clara Novello Davies, mother of Cardiff-born composer Ivor Novello, organised an appeal for musical instruments for the troops in World War Two. In World War One she collected 5,000 mouth-organs and 10,000 tin whistles for soldiers in the trenches.

Barrage balloons were used to help defend Cardiff from German bombers and this group of women were based at Ely. From top to bottom, Norah Upton, Mary Black, Gerry Heasman, Gwen Griffiths and 'Tich'.

A more formal photograph at the Ely Barrage Balloon Depot.

Wartime firemen at East Moors, Cardiff. Leading fireman Idris Jenkins is in the centre of the back row.

The first Auxiliary Fire Service team in Cathays in 1939: Sub officer Edmunds, Bill Cleverley, Idris Jenkins, taxi driver Arthur Gomm, Bob Marshall and Lionel Wiggins.

Insole Court in Llandaff was an operational base for the National Fire Service and here are some of the telephonists, with column officer Nunn, who were based there.

B Company 11th Battalion of Glamorgan Home Guard at their stand-down ceremony at Ely in 1944.

The Home Guard battalion at Guest Keen and Baldwin Steel Works.

Cardiff Docks fire brigade in November 1944.

March past of the Cardiff sector Home Guard at their final parade in Cardiff in 1944.

Field Marshal Viscount Montgomery, who led the British troops to victory in World War Two, visited East Moors Steelworks in May 1954.

A street party in Edward Street, Cardiff in 1945. That's the old Capitol Cinema in the background.

Troops at Cardiff Central Station on the way to the front in World War One.

The date was 17 May 1900 and crowds gathered at the Monument end of St Mary Street as the news broke that the South African town of Mafeking had been relieved after a 207-day siege.

Corps of Drums of the 2nd Battalion Welsh Regiment leaving Cardiff for France in 1916. By April many were killed or wounded.

Troops leaving Cardiff Castle in World War One.

A gun captured by the Welsh Guards in 1915 was presented to the city of Cardiff.

A scene outside Whitchurch Library during World War One.

ENTERTAINERS

A young Shirley Bassey at the Rainbow Club, Bute Street, where she used to sing as a youngster.

Shirley Bassey signing autographs in Cardiff in May 1957.

Shirley Bassey at the Rainbow Club, Cardiff, in May 1957.

Another signing session for Shirley in September 1957.

Bassey back at the Rainbow Club in September 1957.

Cheers for Bassey outside the New Theatre, Cardiff in September 1957.

Cheers for Bassey
outside the New
Theatre, Cardiff in
September 1957.
When the Beatles
came to Cardiff in
1965 they found time
to hang a doll on a
Christmas Tree.

Beatlemania in Cardiff in 1965.

Tom Jones in 1965
when It's Not
Unusual shot from
No. 21 to No. 2 in the
charts in two weeks.

Tom Jones when he passed his driving test in Newport in 1966.

Adoring fans of Tom Jones at the Paget Rooms, Penarth, in 1965.

Cardiff-born Shakin Stevens, in his role as Elvis which he made famous on stage in the 1970s.

The Sybil Marks formation dancing team which represented Cardiff in the BBC's Come Dancing competition in 1970.

Sybil Marks with her dancers rehearsing in 1971.

The Sybil Marks-Phil Williams dancing team which won the BBC Come Dancing challenge cup in 1958.

The music and songs of Cardiff-born composer Ivor Novello still ring around the world. He was born at 95 Cowbridge Road East, Cardiff and is seen here with his mother Madam Clara Novello Davies, who founded the globe-trotting Royal Welsh Ladies' Choir.

Ivor Novello when he was the heart-throb of thousands.

Novello with film star Phyllis Monkman just days before the composer's death at the age of 58 in March 1951.

Cardiff-born 'Two-Ton Tessie' O'Shea made her stage debut in the 1930s and was still in demand as an entertainer in America 60 years later. She died in April 1995.

Tessie on a visit to Cardiff in 1957.

Folk singer Vic Parker who used to entertain the regulars in The Quebec pub in Butetown, Cardiff, before his death in 1978.

Vic Parker's New-Orleans style funeral in Bute Street in 1978.

The BBC voice in Wales for decades was the late Alun Williams seen here with broadcaster and folk singer Frank Hennessy.

Alun Williams and Peter Murray with Deano Wilson, the Ely singer who won television's Opportunity Knocks contest eight weeks on the trot in 1966.

Deano Wilson as a child star. She later emigrated to Canada after quitting the big time.

Deano with Cliff Richard in Cardiff in 1965, before she won Opportunity Knocks.

The Echo published a Cliff Richard Special when the singer visited Cardiff in 1962. With him is Hilary John, of Whitchurch, who a few years later was under siege by the Red Guards at the British Embassy in Peking.

SPORTING MOMENTS

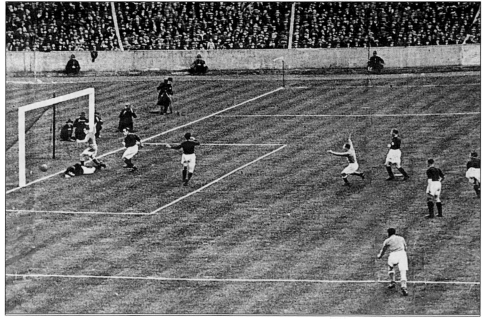

The date 23 April 1927, was the greatest day in the history of Welsh soccer. The day Cardiff City beat Arsenal 1-0 to win the FA Cup at Wembley. The goal was credited to Hugh Ferguson, from near the penalty-spot, but some say Len Davies helped it over the line.

NORTH TERRACE SEATS
(Uncovered)

ENTRANCE

1

ENTER AT TURNSTILES **D**
(SEE PLAN ON BACK)

EMPIRE STADIUM, WEMBLEY

The Football Association
Cup Competition

FINAL TIE

Saturday, April 23rd, 1927
Kick-off 3.0 p.m.

Price 5/-
(including Tax)

Row   Seat

15   4

Joint Liquidators,
British Empire Exhibition.

THIS PART TO BE RETAINED
(See Conditions on back)

The Arsenal fans and the Press blamed goalkeeper Dan Lewis, a Welshman, for the goal.

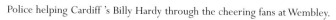

Police helping Cardiff 's Billy Hardy through the cheering fans at Wembley.

Cardiff 's captain Fred Keenor with the cup. Goal hero Ferguson is on the left.

The whole city turned out to welcome the team back to Cardiff.

The Cardiff City team, reserves, directors, officials and staff with the FA Cup.

Future world featherweight boxing champion Howard Winstone, from Merthyr, won gold at the Empire Games in Cardiff in 1958 when he beat G. Taylor of Australia.

Echo compositor Malcolm Collins struck silver at Cardiff in 1958 and in Canada four years later. He is seen in action in Cardiff against Australian, W.Taylor. An outstanding amateur who refused all offers to turn professional, Malcolm won 31 championship bouts with first-round knock-outs.

Malcolm Collins' hand raised in victory after beating Purton, of New Zealand, at Cardiff in 1958.

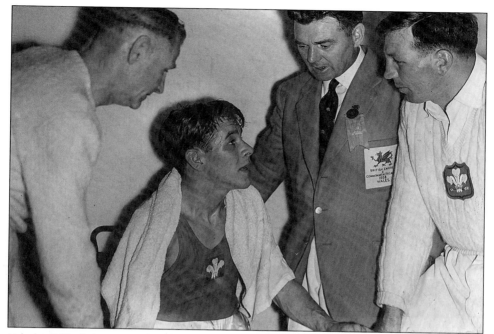

Malcolm Collins being congratulated by team manager John Llewellyn, J.Driscoll and Eddie Thomas.

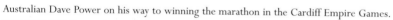

Australian Dave Power on his way to winning the marathon in the Cardiff Empire Games.

Cheers for D.M.Morgan, of Wales, competing against Williams of Scotland in the Empire Games.

One of the world's greatest swimmers, Australian Dawn Fraser, won gold with a new world record in the 110 yards freesytle at the Empire Pool in 1958. The silver went to L.Crapp and the bronze to A.Colquhuon.

The Welsh Ladies Medley Relay Team which made the 1958 final, Geraldine Francis, Joyce Dixon, Gillian Howells and Jocelyn Hooper.

Athletics legend Herb Elliot, of Australia, winning his heat in the mile at Cardiff in 1958.

Welsh fencers John McCombe and Jennifer King.

All smiles at the Empire Games closing ceremony.

Competitors link for Auld Lang Syne at the end of the Games.

Empire Games spectators celebrating the Queen's announcement that Prince Charles was to become Prince of Wales on reaching the age of 21 in 1969.

Mrs H.J. 'Peter' Seaborne checking the uniforms of Welsh competitors at the Empire Games.

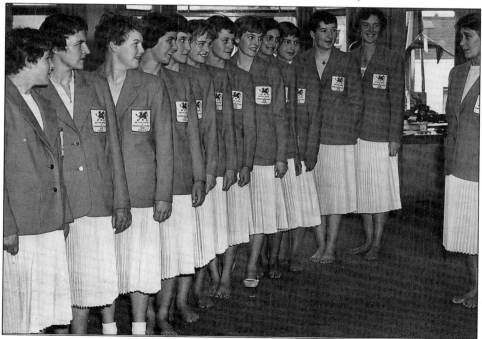

Peerless Jim Driscoll, was king of the boxing world from Edwardian days until after World War One. He did his apprenticeship in the fairground booths and became a featherweight champion of Britain.

Jim Driscoll's mother Elizabeth, with some of her son's trophies. She worked as a docker unloading potatoes at Cardiff.

A boxing battalion in World War One. Back row, Bombardier Billy Wells, Pat O'Keefe, Johnny Basham and Dick Smith. Front row, the 'Mighty Atom', Jimmy Wilde, Capt Bruce Logan and Peerless Jim Driscoll.

Scenes at the funeral of Peerless Jim Driscoll in Cardiff in 1925.

In 1909, Peerless Jim gave up the chance of fighting Abe Atell for the world title because he had promised to box for his favourite charity, Nazareth House, in Cardiff. After his death the Sisters of Nazareth paid for his Celtic Cross headstone, on which he is wrongly described as a featherweight champion of the world. Standing at the grave is former Echo boxing correspondent Bert Allen.

A bare-knuckle fight at the Cow and Snuffers at Llandaff North between landlord George Asplin (left) and Enoch 'Knocker' White. Timekeeper was Dick Long.

The Welsh amateur boxing team given a civic reception by the Lord Mayor of Cardiff before competing in Dublin in 1935.

The teenage Joe Erskine who became the heavyweight boxing champion of Britain and the British Empire. In 1948 Joe was Welsh schoolboy and army cadet champion.

Joe Erskine, Bill Boston and Len Bullen, all of the Cardiff Central Boys' Club, who played for Wales against England in the boys' rugby international at Neath in 1952. Boston became a noted rugby league player with Wigan.

Henry Cooper was beaten on points by Joe Erskine over 15 rounds in 1957.

Joe Erskine is welcomed home to Cardiff after beating Joe Bygraves to win the Empire championship in 1957.

Boxing manager Eddie Thomas kept a watchful eye on Joe Erskine in 1958.

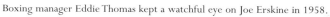

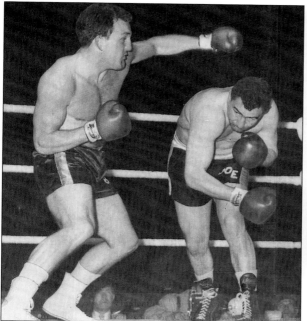

Billy Walker has a close encounter with Joe Erskine at Wembley in 1964.

Jack London fails to land with a punch as Joe Erskine ducks in a 1958 clash.

Rivals Dick Richardson, of Newport and Joe Erskine mix it at Maindy Stadium in 1967. Erskine won on points.

Joe Erskine in training at
his Cardiff gym in 1961.

Cardiff 's history as a boxing
city was crowned when Steve
Robinson won the featherweight championship of the
world in sensational fashion in 1993. He was called in
as a lastminute substitute to fight the holder John
Davison, won the fight and retained the title on a
number of occasions.

The greatest Olympian to be born in Cardiff was
swimmer and water-polo player Paulo Radmilovic
who represented Great Britain in six consecutive
Olympic Games from 1906 to 1928. He won four
Olympic Gold medals for swimming and water polo.

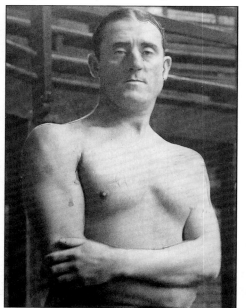

Radmilovic and Valerie Davies being congratulated by the Lord Mayor after being selected to swim for Wales in Canada in 1930.

The Taff Swim was an annual event in Cardiff. The race used to be staged in the river but was switched to Roath Park for health and safety reasons. The scene during a river swim in the 1920s.

Swimmers heading for the Canton Bridge in a pre-war Taff Swim.

Taff swim competitors lined up at Roath Park Lake in 1952.

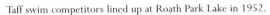

The off! Competitors enter Roath Park for the 1952 Taff Swim.

Some of the women competitors in the Taff Swim in 1959.

Trophy winners in the Taff Swim at Roath Park in 1959. Sitting on the right was Frank Webber, managing director of the Western Mail & Echo. Standing left are Jack Wiggins and Tom Coakley, the then editor and circulation manager of the Echo.

Competitors in the Taff Swim in 1939 included John Parkman, who later became head of the Regional Crime Squad in South Wales, and Echo journalist and librarian Ted Browning.

Thirty-one years after his Taff Swim plunge, John Parkman is seen with fellow policemen at his retirement party.

Jenny James, of Pontypridd, was the greatest long-distance swimmer produced by Wales. In the 1940s and 1950s she swam both the Bristol and English Channels as well as some of the greatest lakes. With her father she is seen talking to the driver of the train which took her to Dover for a 1950 swim.

Jenny James at the Cardiff Ladies' Swimming Club after swimming the Bristol Channel in 1949.

Jenny James swimming the Bristol Channel in 1949.

Cardiff's Martyn Woodroffe arriving home from from the Mexico Olympics where he won a silver medal in the breaststroke swim in 1968.

Woodroffe gets a welcome home kiss from his sister Judith at Cardiff General Station.

While in Mexico, Martyn had his watch stolen so his neighbours on the Pentrebane Estate had a whip-round to buy him a new one.

Canton High School headmaster Harold Davies sent congratulations to pupil Martyn Woodroffe after his silver swim in Mexico.

The Welsh rugby team which played in a Victory international in Paris in 1946. The three at the front are Hubert Jones, Cliff Davies and W.J.Evans. Also included in the picture are Billy Cleaver, Bleddyn Williams, Jack Matthews, Les Manfield and D.J.Davies, the father of 'Merve the Swerve'.

Cardiff's Billy Cleaver in action against England at Twickenham in 1946.

Cliff Davies, Les Manfield and Maldwyn James are among the Welshmen in this clash with England at Twickenham in 1948.

Cardiff's legendary scrum-half Haydn Tanner playing against France in 1947.

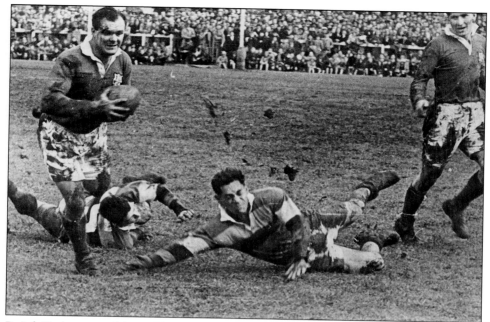

Dr Jack Matthews, one of the Cardiff greats of all time, playing for the British Lions against Hamilton in New Zealand in 1950.

The Glamorgan team that won the County Cricket Championship in 1948. Standing (left to right): Willie Jones, Phil Clift, Norman Hever, Stan Trick, William Parkhouse, J.T. Eaglestone, Jim Pleass. Seated: G. Lavis, wicketkeeper Hadyn Davies, J.C. Clay, Wilf Wooller, E. Davies, Len Muncer and Alan Watkins.

World War Two veteran Dave Winters became a sporting legend, although confined to a wheelchair for over 50 years. He was a patient at Rookwood Hospital, Cardiff, and represented Wales in many paraplegic sports, including Commonwealth level. He is seen here with John Gronow, another Welsh international.

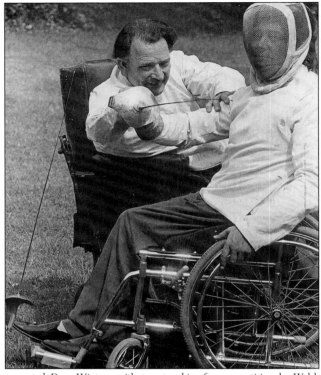

In 1968, Cardiff City Social Club presented Dave Winters with two trophies for competition by Welsh paraplegic sports people.

Cardiff's wheelchair athlete Tanni Grey struck gold with outstanding performances in the Paraplegic Olympics in Barcelona.

Joyce White, of Victoria Park, returned to Cardiff in triumph after winning two gold and a silver medal swimming for Britain in the Special Olympics (for Downs Syndrome People) in New York in the 1970s. At the station to greet her was Pipe Major Bob Murphy, from St Patrick's Pipe Band.

Ely Racecourse, a popular sporting venue up to the 1930s.

Greyhound racing ended at the Cardiff Arms Park in the 1970s. The winner of the Welsh Greyhound Derby in 1962 was Summerhill Fancy, trained by George Waterman, holding the trophy.

The Cardiff 100 Miles Road Club in 1897. The club was formed to encourage cyclists to pedal 100 miles in 12 hours.

Wales is credited with introducing baseball to the Americans. This was one of Cardiff's greatest players, Freddie Fish, in action against England at Sophia Gardens.

A bowling match at Penhill, Cardiff, in Edwardian days.

The Cardiff Olympic Youth Club gymnastic team that won the British team championship in 1958. Denise Goddard, Joan Richards, coach Bob Davies, Mary McCarthy and Margaret Neale.

St Saviour's Gymnastic team, winners of the Welsh championships in 1911.

POLITICIANS

James Taylor, 91, was the first person in 1945 to cast his vote in Cardiff South East for Jim Callaghan, who rose through the Labour ranks to become Prime Minister.

In 1947, Jim Callaghan met members of the Colonial Club, Cardiff, to tell them about a recent visit he had made to Africa.

Just testing, Jim Callaghan at Adamsdown Park, Cardiff, in 1947.

Jim Callaghan chaired by supporters after being re-elected in 1950.

Phillip Noel-Baker, Minister of Fuel and Power, and Jim Callaghan at a Splott fête in the early 1950s. The carnival queen was Maureen Riley.

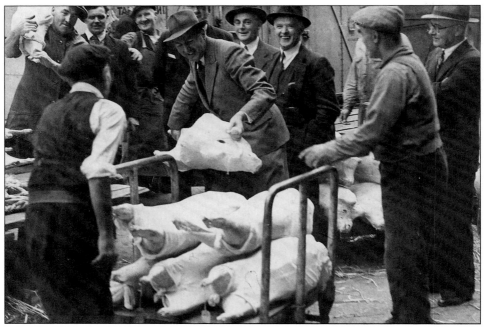

Pleased to meat you! Jim Callaghan at the Cardiff cold stores in 1951.

Young supporters of Jim Callaghan in 1955.

Dancing the twist at Sophia Gardens in 1963 are Jim Callaghan and Pamela Winn, of Roath, Cardiff.

Grangetown boys Ken Stoeman, Ian Stewart and David Jones give the thumbs-up to Jim Callaghan and his wife Audrey in 1965.

Jim Callaghan visiting Newtown, Cardiff, in 1964.

When he was Chancellor of the Exchequer in 1964, Jim Callaghan found time to watch Cardiff City. His hosts were City manager Jimmy Scoular, chairman Fred Dewey and former Welsh international George Edwards.

Jim Callaghan was all smiles at the Ocean Club, Tremorfa, in 1964. With him are Peggy Brooks, Marita Matthewson, Pam Groves, the future MP Rhodri Morgan and Jannette Carter.

Jim Callaghan was Foreign Secretary when he was knocking on the door of No 10 Downing Street in 1964. He was Prime Minister from 1976 to 1979.

The MP for Cardiff West, George Thomas, became Speaker of the House of Commons before being named a viscount for his services to politics. Here he is seen talking to pensioners in Ely in 1964. They were complaining about having to queue at local post offices.

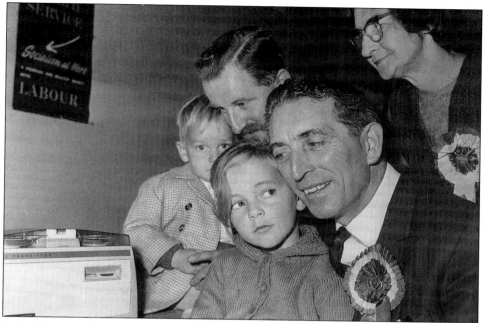

A taped-message wishing him good luck was made for George Thomas in 1964 by six-year-old Sylvia Walters. Also listening to the tape are Mr E.R. Walters, his son David and Olwen Parry, who was the MP's agent.

George Thomas' greatest achievement as an MP was to get a Leasehold Reform Bill through Parliament. He is seen here with some of the people who signed a petition he launched.

Ann Rees, dressed in an election outfit, was greeted by George Thomas when she voted at Ninian Park School in 1970.

In 1963 George Thomas was challenged in the Commons for wearing an Old Etonian tie. "I bought it in the Co-op in Tonypandy," he told MPs.

George Thomas had a great devotion to his mother, affectionately known to politicians as 'Mam'.

A relaxing moment at the Golden Jubilee Celebrations at St Illtyd's College, Cardiff, in 1973. From the left, Brother Alexander, Archbishop John Murphy, Sir Charles Hallinan, George Thomas, Jim Callaghan, Brother Victor and Bishop Daniel Mullins.

Winston Churchill in St Mary Street, Cardiff, when he was given the Freedom of the City in 1948.

Cheers for Churchill on his drive through Cardiff in 1948.

A Churchillian blessing for patients and staff at the Prince of Wales Hospital, near the Mansion House, in 1948.

Churchill and his son-in-law Christopher Soames arriving in Cardiff in 1948.

Churchill at an election rally at Ninian Park in 1950.

One man and his dog. Michael Foot, MP for Ebbw Vale and later leader of the Labour Party, at a miners gala in Cardiff in 1966. Next to him is Dai Francis, South Wales secretary of the National Union of Mineworkers.

Cardiff Conservative MP Donald Box dealing with a problem after flooding in Gabalfa in 1963.

Pontypool's MP Leo Abse's budget day outfits always raised a smile. In 1961 the Cardiff solicitor wore a brown Van Dyck stove-pipe hat, a stone-coloured suit, cut in Edwardian style, a sepia waistcoat and an orchid buttonhole.

South Wales MPs united in the battle to save the steel industry in 1973, Raymond Gower, George Thomas, Arthur Probert, Jim Callaghan, Fred Evans and Michael Roberts.

Conservative Minister of Transport, Ernest Marples, reading an Echo demand for action to clear the traffic jams from Cardiff streets in 1964. The next day he announced that work would soon start on Eastern Avenue. The reporter was John O'Sullivan.

RELIGION

Pope John Paul II being greeted by the Lord Lieutenant of Glamorgan, Sir Cenydd Traherne and a number of bishops at Cardiff Wales Airport on 2 June 1982.

The Pope arriving at Pontcanna for the Papal Mass.

A nun from Nazareth House has the Pope in view.

A message for the Pope at the Youth Mass at Ninian Park.

Welcoming smiles for the Pope from Zoe Hassan, Baindu Foday, Anne Marie Foday and Nancy Foday, from St Cuthbert's Parish, Cardiff.

Some of the thousands who gathered in Cardiff Castle grounds for the Corpus Christi Benediction service in 1964.

Roman Catholics in Cardiff have held annual Corpus Christi celebrations for more than 100 years. This was part of the procession on the way to the castle grounds in 1911.

Happy pupils of St David's School, Cardiff, in 1964.

St Alban's Band played at Corpus Christi celebrations for decades. Band leader John Williams, seen here with his son and grandson, was involved with the band for more than 60 years.

Archbishop John Murphy arriving at St David's Cathedral, Cardiff, for his enthronement on 31 October 1961.

Wales' greatest Welsh language writer and broadcaster, Saunders Lewis, with Cardinal John Heenan and Archbishop John Murphy at Cardiff in 1961.

Canon Tom Phelan
was a familiar figure
on his bike in his
parish of St Patrick's
Grangetown for
many years.

Llandaff Cathedral Choir, 1914. In the centre of the second row is the future Archdeacon, the Revd James Rice Buckley, whose statue is now a landmark on the Cathedral Green.

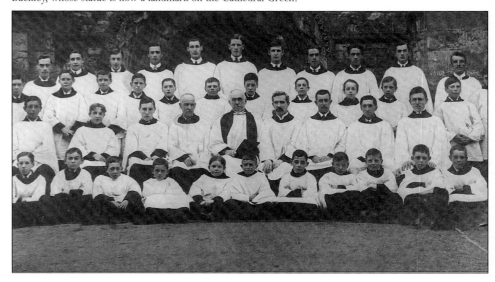

Epstein's Majesty of Christ dominates Llandaff Cathedral at a service in 1960.

The Llandaff Scout Group outside the cathedral in the early 1920s.

In 1923 a Big Tent mission was held on spare ground in Westgate Street. Houses in the Old Temperance Town, where the Echo office now stands, can be seen in the background.

The last meeting at the Salvation Army's Stuart Hall, in Bute Street, Cardiff, took place in May, 1965.

Some of the men who were fed by the Salvation Army at their hostel in Bute Street in the 1960s.

An Easter service at the Greek Orthodox Church in Cardiff in 1959.

The opening of the Peel Street Mosque, Cardiff in 1947.

A Muslim Union's All-world conference was held at the Peel Street Mosque in 1949.

The leader of the Islamia Allaouis religious society, Sheikh Mohamed el Mehdi, of Algiers (centre) visited South Wales in 1954. Others outside the Sophia Street Mosque, Cardiff, (left to right), Sheikh Mohamed Said, Sheikh Hassan Ismail, Sheikh el Mackudam Ahmed and Sheikh Hag Salah.

Celebrating the end of Ramadan, the Moslem month of fasting, in Cardiff, in 1966.

Children leading the procession to mark the end of Ramadan in Cardiff in 1967.

Muslim schoolteacher Saleh Hassan talking to children at the end of the 1967 Ramadan.

Sikhs at a service at their Temple in Riverside, Cardiff.

Charananjit Singh conducting a service at the Sikh Temple.

ROYAL VISITS AND EISTEDDFODS

The Queen and Prince Philip brought Prince Anne and Prince Charles to Cardiff for the National Eisteddfod in 1960.

The Proclamation ceremony at Cardiff Castle in 1959 for the National Eisteddfod held in the city the following year.

The 1959 Proclamation ceremony.

The Gorsedd procession in Queen Street, in 1960.

Welsh exiles being welcomed to the Eisteddfod in 1960.

The Eisteddfod choir, conducted by Arwel Hughes, rehearsing in in 1960.

Cardiff Corporation band at the 1960 Eisteddfod.

The Melingriffith band at the 1960 Eisteddfod.

A scene from the National Eisteddfod in Cardiff in 1938.

GALA DAYS

There was only one working major pit in South Wales in 1995, Tower Colliery at Hirwaun, but King Coal ruled the area for decades before the run-down of the industry which helped to make Cardiff a city. Miners from the valley towns and villages flocked to the capital for the annual gala days, like this one in 1967.

The galas were occasions for all types of protest.

The seamen made their views known at the 1966 gala.

A heckler gets some frosty looks at the 1967 gala.

Listening to the speeches in 1966.

Gala days were also family fun days. This jazz band came from the Ogwr area.

The Echo sponsored the miners' road race in Cardiff in 1926, the year of the General Strike.

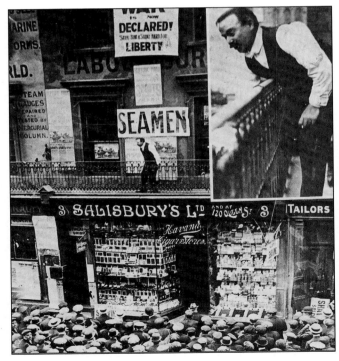

Seamen on strike in Cardiff in 1911.

Hunger marchers camped at Leckwith Common in the early part of the 20th century.

BY AIR AND LAND

An airship made at Cardiff by Ernest Willows flies past the City Hall in 1910.

Willows at the controls of his airship.

Charles Watkins, of Colum Road, Cardiff, built and flew this machine around 1910 when he was only 19 years of age. He said he was the first man to fly over Cardiff at night. This photograph was taken in the 1960s.

The old monoplane was kept in a garage at Blackweir, Cardiff for decades, until Charles Watkins donated it to the RAF museum at St Athan, where he is seen polishing the machine in 1967.

Charles Watkins also designed and built this electric driven car which was capable of speeds up to 25mph. It was 7ft long.

A Taff Vale engine in Victorian times.

The Taff Vale Railway Station near the site of Queen Street Station in Cardiff, in the 1850s.

The Taff Vale engine used when the Prince of Wales visited the Cardiff Industrial and Fine arts Exhibition in Cardiff in 1896.

In 1907 the Twamley brothers delivered coal at five old pence a hundredweight to the seamen's lodging houses in Tiger Bay.

A horse-drawn bus which plied between Cardiff and Penarth in the late 19th century.

A paraffin seller trading in Cardiff in the 19th century. The boy in the cart was William Down, of Roath. The man was George Eveleigh and the other lad Jack White.

A horse-drawn tram in Grangetown, Cardiff.

The Canton to Docks bus in Severn Road in 1896.

A Cardiff Corporation Transport vehicle in the 19th century.

The first Cardiff trams arriving at Newport Road in 1900. They started operating in the city on 1 May 1902.

The trams were truly launched when the Japanese Navy came to Cardiff in August 1902.

This was the first motor bus to operate in Cardiff from 1910.

This was the bus that operated between Cardiff and Whitchurch in 1922.

One of these 1916 conductresses was Gladys Redmond, of Howell Road, Ely, Cardiff.

Driver Frank Smith and conductor George Evans with a Cardiff to Whitchurch bus in 1921.

The Riches company operated this vehicle from 1910 to 1915.

The Adamsdown Labour Party setting off on an outing in the 1920s.

Leaving the City Hall on an outing in 1926.

Cloth caps and buttonholes were the order of the day in 1928.

This group left the Splott Conservative Club in 1928.

The end of an era. The last tram journey in Cardiff on 20 February 1950.

Conductress Hetty Clarke collecting fares when trolley buses were introduced in Cardiff in 1950.

Guy Forrest with his Napier taxi outside the Taff Station in Cardiff in 1916.

Members of the Splott Labour Club made history when they charted an aeroplane to fly them from Pengam aerodrome to watch the 1937 Rugby League Cup Final at Wembley. The total cost of hiring two seven-seater planes was only £32!

Four people were killed when a pleasure plane from the Ideal Home Exhibition crashed near Cardiff High School, in North Road, Cardiff on 13 May 1959.

Sifting through the wreckage of the plane after the North Road crash.

An AA man from Cardiff at the Storey Arms during the blizzards in 1963.

Clearing the snow in Clifton Street, Roath, in 1963.

The Monument end of St Mary Street in 1963.

Llanrumney under 3ft of snow in 1963.

Slushy route from the bus station in 1963.

Neville Street when the Taff burst its banks in 1961.

Cowbridge Road in the 1961 floods.

A horse-drawn fire tender was the only machine available to firefighters in Cardiff in the middle of the 19th century.

A Cardiff fireboat operating on the old Glamorganshire Canal around 1912.

A fireboat giving a demonstration at Cardiff Docks around 1912.

One of the first police cars introduced into Cardiff in 1934 was driven by PC John Gale.

John Gale on point duty near Cardiff Castle in the 1930s.

THE DOCKS

Women dockers unloading potatoes from a ship at Cardiff Docks in the late 19th century.

An early picture of Cardiff Docks, from the archives of the South Wales branch of the World Ship Society.

Cardiff-Penarth Ferry boats, at Cardiff around 1890, including the Kate (1865), La Belle Marie (1866) and Iona (1883).

Cardiff Docks at the turn of the century when it was the greatest coal exporting port in the world.

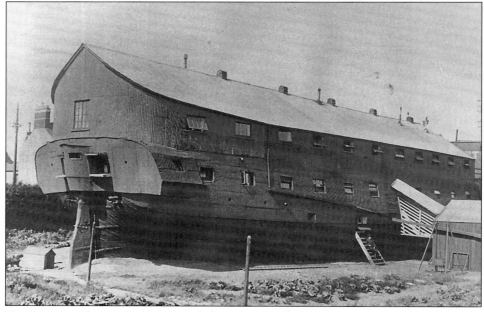

The Havannah, a former 42-gun frigate, which escorted Napoleon Bonaparte to exile on the island of St Helena, served as an industrial school at Cardiff Docks for 40 years up to 1905.

The Hamadryad, another former Naval ship, was used as a hospital at Cardiff in Victorian times. A hospital bearing the same name was later built in Cardiff.

The figurehead of HMS Hamadryad was placed in the Hamadryad Hospital at Cardiff Docks where it is being admired by student nurse Mary Willis.

Another reminder of when Cardiff was a bustling coal exporting port.

Paddle steamers at Cardiff in Edwardian days.

This was all that was left of a tug which was destroyed by an explosion which killed five men in 1886.

This photograph of the Royal Navy Mothball Fleet at Cardiff was taken from an aircraft in 1954 by the late Les Grist, Echo photographer.

Guests at the opening of Fletchers Wharf, Roath Dock, Cardiff, in 1966.

Repair gang in dry docks at Cardiff in 1967.

The steel industry in Cardiff was run down in the 1970s. This was a mass meeting at East Moors when the men voted to fight to try to save the works from closure.

It was no laughing matter, but there were still many smiles.

CITY OF TRADES

Staff at the building site of the Andrews Empire taken on 22 August 1891. Solomon Andrew is third from the left in the front.

Blacksmith Richard White and two strikers working in a forge in the late 19th century.

Workers outside Rumney Bridge Pottery in Victorian times.

A messy job inside the Rumney pottery in 1960.

This picture of Fred Lewis, inspecting one of the many tunnels which carry Cardiff 's sewage, was taken by Echo photographer John Hawken in 1968.

Arthur Wiseman uses his Davy lamp to test for gas before proceeding into the tunnels with Fred Lewis.

Making basket chairs at Cardiff Institute for the Blind which opened in late Victorian days.

Some of the earliest workers at the Institute for the Blind.

EDUCATION

The Victorian Infants School in the Hayes, the archway on the left led to where Cardiff's first electric light was installed.

Pupils at Roath Village School in 1899. Notice the cane in the teacher's hands.

Pupils at Severn Road Girls School, Canton, in 1907.

Lining up in the yard of Crwys Road School, Cardiff around 1913.

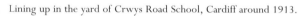

Surrounded by plants are pupils of Radnor Road School, Canton, in 1903 when the teacher was a Miss Gibbons.

The man with the dog was the 'whipper-in' or truancy officer at Cathays National School in the early 1880s. To keep the boys in order he formed the Cathays Pipe and Drum band.

Pupils and teachers at St David's School, Cardiff, in Victorian times.

Rumney Council School, 1919.

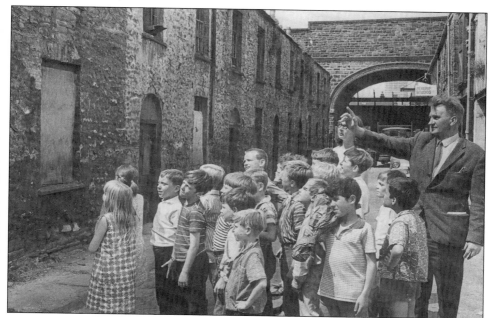

One of Cardiff's greatest historians, Bill Barrett, was with this group of children from Moorland Junior School, Cardiff in 1969 when they stumbled across these 1830s cottages near Bute Street.

The Church Lads Brigade lined up at Howard Gardens, Cardiff in 1910.

Girl Guides of the 4th Cardiff Company at New Trinity Church, Canton, in 1918.

In 1950 these Docks children set up a school on the site of the Hamadryad Hospital.

Children playing on a dump near Harrowby Street, Cardiff Docks, in 1959.

Three boys paddle across the old Cardiff West Dock on their homemade canoe.

Fishing in the Timber Pond at Cardiff, Jean Maegusku, William Bualch, Robert Craven and Richard Clifton.

BUTETOWN

Butetown Health Centre in 1969.

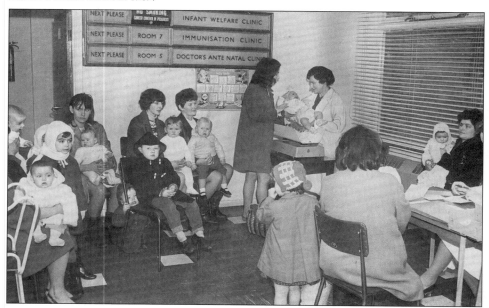

Residents of South Church Street, concerned over eviction notices in 1967.

Pat Rees and her children were the last residents in Patrick Street, Docks, when it was being demolished in 1969.

SHOPPING

In September 1963 Garratts, in Working Street, Cardiff, sold dresses and coats for around three old pence each following a fire at the store.

Queuing for bargains at Cross Brothers Store in the Hayes, Cardiff, during an 'reconstruction sale' in 1964.

A shopping revolution came to Cardiff in the early 1960s with the first supermarkets, but the location of this one was not included in the caption.

Seccombes Stores stood on the corner of Park Place and Queen Street when this picture of the staff was taken in the 1930s. All of the 200 employees received a week's pay for every year of service in the will of their former boss, T.P. Webber.

Two famous shop names
in Cardiff were 'married'
in the 20th century as
can be seen from this
picture of the Bon
Marche and Seccombes
in Queen Street.

Generations of Cardiffians looked for
bargains in Grimwades in Cowbridge
Road, Canton.

In 1970 Michael Asprou feared his shop in Bute Street was going to be demolished. He won his fight and formed a holiday company which was sold in the early 1990s. It made his family, including his son Dimitrie – in the picture – millionaires.

GYPSIES

Until a permanent site was provided for caravan dwellers in Rover Way, Cardiff in the 1960s, there was a constant battle between gypsies and the authorities who moved them on. Lydia Lee was Queen of the Gypsies in the city and she said she had paid enough fines to have bought Queen Street.

A wedding feast for a young gypsy couple in June 1966.

It was not unusual to see a horse-drawn Romany caravan like this at Leckwith Common in the 1950s.

CIVIC AFFAIRS

Cardiff Corporation's annual visit to the Taff Fawr Waterworks in the Brecon Beacons in 1890.

The first meeting of Cardiff City Council, 23 October 1905.

The official opening of the Lewis Samuel Fountain in Splott in 1909.

The digging of Splott Baths in the early 1920s.

The opening of Splott Baths on 14 August 1922.

The civic party arriving at Cardiff Castle in 1947 when the Bute family presented the castle to the city.

Lord Mayor W.J.H. Muston reading the result of the poll in 1952, when Cardiff voted in favour of opening cinemas on a Sunday.

The scene in the civic centre in 1955, when it was announced that Cardiff was the Capital City of Wales.

HOSPITALS

A horse-drawn ambulance at the Isolation Hospital in Landsdowne Road earlier this century.

Staff at Whitchurch Hospital, Cardiff, in the 1920s.

The Roath Furnishing Company presented items to Cardiff Royal Infirmary in 1932.

Just three of the children born in Cardiff hospitals: the Horwood triplets, Cheryl, Adrian and Sally, celebrating their sixth birthday in Cardiff on 4 July 1967. Cardiff has one of the most active multiple birth clubs in Britain.

STREET SCENES

The James family of Clodien Avenue, Cardiff, strolling in King Edward VII Avenue, Cardiff, in 1900.

Kingsway, Cardiff, in Edwardian days.

Queen Street, Cardiff, towards the end of the 19th century.

The Glamorganshire Canal and Mill Lane, Cardiff.

Another view of the canal.

The Greyfriars ruins which stood on the site where the Pearl Building now stands in Greyfriars Road.

The Westgate Street flats under construction in 1936.

Newtown, Cardiff, before it was demolished in the mid-1960s.

Albany Road, Roath, in 1963.

The old bridge and cottage at the bottom of Leckwith Hill.

A court known as Irish Row was near the site of the Queen's Hotel in St Mary Street. The court was demolished in 1889.

The junction of Wood Street and St Mary Street in 1962.

A view of Wood Street before Temperance Town was demolished in the 1930s.

Temperance Town before it was bulldozed in the 1930s. The *Echo* office now stands on part of the site.

Another view of Temperance Town after the demolition contractors moved in in 1933. The cleared area is what is now Wood Street.

The chaos at the corner of Wood Street and Westgate Street after a rugby international in the early 1970s.

This was Cardiff High Street in 1869.

The Hayes around the turn of the century. The Old Central Library was built on the site of the building on the right.

Duke Street, 1877. The gateway is where the main entrance to Cardiff Castle is now situated. The buildings were where the Castle Green moat was created. The gabled house was the office of the Marquis of Bute's solicitor.

Another view of Duke Street before the shops on the north side were demolished to make way for the Castle Green.

Kingsway, Cardiff, in 1887. The bus shelters now occupy the site of the building on the left, which was the Savings Bank. There is no clue to the youngsters' identity.

Hackney cabs were introduced into Cardiff around 1859 and were a popular form of transport in the Victorian and early Edwardian days. The Borough Arms has changed little from the outside since this picture was taken.

St Mary Street in the 1920s, showing the Wireless College above the entrance to Cardiff Market. It was from here in 1921 that the first 'radio' concert in the world was broadcast. Violinist Garforth Mortimer played a variety of tunes which were relayed to an invited audience at the Cory Hall which was opposite Queen Street Station. The audience used headphones to listen in.

The Duke of Clarence came to Cardiff in 1890 to officially open Clarence Bridge, linking Grangetown with Butetown.

Parking was no problem in Cathays Park in 1931.

A fleet of chauffeur-driven cars lined up near the Synagogue in Cathedral Road in the early part of this century.

Queen Street, Cardiff, before World War One. The Park Hotel is still standing but the rest of the street has changed dramatically. The cinema on the left is where the first talkie movies were shown in the city in the late 1920s.

The corner of Queen Street and Churchill Way, when the canal was fenced off.

William Lewis standing outside the Cyfartha offices in West Wharf in Victorian times.

The Turnpike Gate between Llantrisant Road and Road Bridge, Llandaff. Tolls had to be paid by riders of horse-drawn vehicles before the Turnpike was demolished around 1890.

The original bridge across the River Taff, linking Bridge Road with Llandaff North. It was built in 1770. The photograph was taken before 1890 when the bridge was widened and iron lattice work added.

A No 24 bus crossing Llandaff Bridge, possibly in the 1940s. The bridge was virtually swept away by flood water on 27 December 1979.

Whitchurch Village as seen from the bell tower of St Mary's Church in 1897. The Plough Inn, on the corner of Merthyr Road and Old Church Road, is still a landmark in the area.